EPICS:
Cloud Included

S. E. McKenzie

DEDICATION

To everyone who has been left out in the cold

THIS BOOK IS A BOOK OF SPECULATIVE FICTION.
Characters, companies, governments, places, events, are either
products of the author's imagination or used fictitiously. Any
resemblance to persons (living or dead), companies, governments,
places and/or events, is a coincidence.

CONTENTS

S.E. McKENZIE

LOST
IN THE FOG

#1. LOST IN THE FOG

I

I heard Mark Bow screaming,
No, I was not dreaming.
For he was begging for mercy

Hoping that the king would hear
For the king was always out of sight,
So Mark Bow begged with all his might.

Even as the sun
Was setting
He never stopped begging.

He begged for mercy
All through the night,
But the king did not hear a word;

Mark Bow did not have that right.
Even though
Mark Bow was not yet dead.

And Mark Bow said:

"Please dear King
Give the command
And free me from this tree,

So that I can return
To my true love,
My beautiful Marie.

Yes, I missed roll call,
That is very true
But I never would have deserted

A kind king like you."

II

In days gone past
He rode as fast
As his horse Charge

Could trot
For the dead were lying
All around
Their bodies were left to rot.

EPICS: Cloud Included

As their spirits were floating away,

I heard Mark Bow say:
"I have been just one of many
Lost at sea that day,

I should have been more aware,
And I am sorry for this fault.
The fog spread through the sky,

While torrents rained angrily,
I was being rocked
In the arms of my true love

My beautiful Marie.

The waves too rocked my ship
So how was I to know
That my ship had been carried

So far away from shore,
While I was sleeping peacefully
Upon the ship's floor,

With my beautiful Marie?

Please kind King
Free me from this tree,
I am not your enemy,

For I was freely giving
My loyalty to you every day,
And I know you will miss my servitude

If you let me die this way.

So don't let me die this way!

You see, I must be free,
To return to my true love,
My beautiful Marie.

III

I have crossed the line
Between Heaven and Earth
Many times for you, dear King

EPICS: Cloud Included

So please give out the command
Which could free me
From this tree,

For I carry this ring
Meant for the hand
Of my true love

My beautiful Marie.

A promise is made to keep,
So don't let me die this way,
For I must return as soon as I can

To my beautiful Marie.

My true love is willing and living,
So I have never been less ready to die;
I force my will to keep my weary eyes open,

And my heart pounding as I try not to cry,
Though I feel so weak and very sad.
If I didn't believe in this love so grand,

I would let myself fade away
Into the unknown,
Because I feel so bad.

Somewhere between
Heaven and Earth
I hang here from this tree,

Hoping the force of your crown,
Can set me free,
Without letting me down;

So that I can follow my chosen path
Into tomorrow
With my true love by my side."

And the king did not know Mark Bow
For Mark Bow was the same
As any other man with any other name.

Even though many men said
That the king's days
Were numbered

EPICS: Cloud Included

The king denied feeding off the poor
And said that he was just the same
As other kings ruling from before.

And many were pushed
Into heaven's revolving door,
Into a world where they would yearn no more.

As the time went by,
Mark Bow's future grew bleaker,
As he grew weaker.

And Mark Bow said:

"I awoke and saw,
Three black birds of prey,
Taking refuge on my ship that day.

They were blown away
By the wind so strong,
Just like me and my beautiful Marie.

While the storm grew
And the wind blew
We too were lost at sea.

So please forgive me.

IV

The Earth's power
Surrounded me with mist
And that is the reason why

When my sergeant called out
My name from the list
I was not there to reply.

So my sergeant declared
Me missing
While I was still kissing

My true love
My beautiful
Marie.

I just want to say

That going AWOL
Was never part of any plan;
So please kind King

EPICS: Cloud Included

I must believe so I don't fade away
That I will be free
Before I die

And I have already told you why
I need to return
To my true love,

My beautiful Marie.

V

As I hang from this tree
I see the clouds above
As I remember my true love,

My beautiful Marie.

I must return to her,
And stay close by her side,
For as long as I am still alive.

So kind King,
Grant me the right to stay living,
Now that I have found a new world

Which is so loving and giving,

And this life should stay mine
So that I may share it
With my true love

My beautiful Marie."

VI
Though Mark Bow was a captain

And never a knight;
He had fought with vigour,
And had never lost a fight.

And then Mark Bow said:
"They say I deserted my post,
And that is not true,

I was lost at sea
With my true love,
My beautiful Marie.

EPICS: Cloud Included

While we were lost in the fog,
Trapped between Heaven and Earth
We lost track of time

Though, it was no fault of mine.
Oh kind King, shed mercy upon me
Don't let me die this way

For I did return to shore
With a diamond ring
For my true love

My beautiful Marie."

And then Mark Bow said:
"Oh kind King
Of days gone by,

Please cut me down from this tree.
For I am almost dead,
And I must stay living,

For I promised to wed,
My true love,
My beautiful Marie.

I must return to her
For my life is now hers,
Not yours nor mine.

VII

I know Marie is waiting
For the day I can take her hand.
That day could be any day,

Just send out the command."

Then Mark Bow cried out in pain,
Sounding almost insane,
And then he said:

"The Fog sometimes blocks out the light
And can happen any time of day
As the wind blew suddenly

The boat and me and Marie
Drifted away,
And sealed my F

EPICS: Cloud Included

And Mark Bow said:
"I returned as soon as I could,
And I did what

So please dear King set me free,

So I may return
To my horse and sword,
And my beautiful Marie.

My sword is sharp,
My horse is young,
And I am fit.

So I should be busy
Doing this thing
Called war;

And I would never
Abandon my post,
For my life exists as long

As you remain my willing host.

So dear King, please set me free,
So I may return to my true love,
My beautiful Marie."

VIII
And Mark Bow said:
"I was never born to be
So alone it is true,

I was born to be with
My True Love
My beautiful Marie."

And Mark Bow said:
"Marie was my reason for living
For she was so trusting and forgiving;

And what will I do
Without my true love
Empowering my Soul?

For that love
Would generate
Electricity and e

EPICS: Cloud Included

Whenever I felt faint.

That energy surrounded me,
So deeply and freely,
It astounded me,

Made me feel so free,
Which is why I must return to my true love,
My beautiful Marie.

IX

The war around me
Generates opposing sides,
Both wronged in blood,

Both sides forced to crawl in mud."

X

Then Mark Bow said:
"They say I deserted my post
And that is not true

I was just lost at sea
With my true love,
My beautiful Marie.

And under the stars
The sea trapped us within its tides,
And for a moment we were free from wars,

Until we were swept upon these shores.

XI

Now all the death
Surrounding me
Too sad to see and speak of

Made spirits free
To fly from Earth
Into the Heavens above.

When it is my turn
To rest in eternal sleep,
I hope to keep

My heart music
Pure enough to share,
With my true love,

EPICS: Cloud Included

My beautiful Marie.
I will play a melody,
And she will sing along,

And as long as we are together
Our hearty song
Will be hummed in the heavens above for ever."

And Mark Bow said:
"I have seen so much sorrow,
And I don't know what to do,

As I walked among the dead,
I knew the fog could see what was really true;
Like a ghost needing a host just to stay alive.

Just like a ghost

With nothing left to lose,
The fog will cover broken bones,
With the help of morning dew.

Too many broken hearts
With no beat left to pound,
Fighting men, left all alone

To sleep on this soggy ground.
Why do I go on fighting?
So rich men have a throne.

I am forced to fight this war
While my true love Marie,
Is left crying all alone.

If I had my way,"
I heard Mark Bow say
"I would turn all these weapons

Into plowshares and I would do it right away."

XII
And then I heard Mark Bow say

EPICS: Cloud Included

"Fate is not mine to know.
And through my sorrow,
My dreams may appear tomorrow,

Still covered in fog,
Hiding the spectrum of light,
So the rainbow cannot be seen.

XIII

Some wondered where the dead were buried,
Wearing boots as they lay in satin;
The fog was just like a cloud,

Floating above the ground
While the dead
Could not hear a sound;

The skin drum
Kept pounding
Inside me

For this was Life.

XIV

And I was so thankful,
That I had been lost at sea,
With my true love,
My beautiful Marie.

XV

The living awoke
To a new day.
So they arose.

As the fog lingered
All around
Like a ghost

Shadows replaced lives
Now lost in the past
Cursed to float within the will

Of those warm currents
As they waved me so gently
I was so glad to know a time

EPICS: Cloud Included

When I was lost at sea,
With my true love,
My beautiful Marie,

Where silent echoes
Of haunted screams
Were hiding in living streams,

And feeding the land
Living water
So tomorrow could grow

If not lost.

XVI

I see the sun come out at last,
The light shines just like a spec,
On what remains, I can't reflect,

For there were not many gains
Earned on this plot of Earth,
Growing further apart from Heaven,

Violence was implied but never shown;
Better that way,
I heard the sergeant say;

If we lie
While they die
They will never know.

So another day went by:
Some laughed,
Some cried,

Some dominated with hate,
And caused a scene
Just to be mean.

EPICS: Cloud Included

And after the instigation:

Many died,
While I remembered the days lost at sea
With my true love

My beautiful Marie."

XVII
Hoping for a better day
He knew he had to find
A better way.

As Mark Bow hung in the tree
All he could think of was Marie
And all the times that he would never see;

Mark Bow cried out in his pain
"There is so much to gain
So why must I lose it all?

Without better foresight
For the common man
This kingdom is bound to fall."

XVIII

And Mark Bow said:
"I am so confused
I feel that I have been used.

There are hypocrites
All over the place
And they will trespass on you.

If they can, like a big man,
In a game
That only kings can win.

My body aches
But never breaks
As far as I can tell;

I am still living somewhere between
Heaven and Earth
And Hell."

And the rainbow
Is seldom seen
Until after the rain

EPICS: Cloud Included

So it is hard to explain
Especially when the storm spirit
Appeared so rudely

And swiped me and Marie away
With the force of the tide's sway
Without thought to logistics for my success.

The storm spirit
Changed my fate,
Made me late

For the game where only
Peasant kings can win,
As the sea cursed me in its stormy way.

Now I appear
To have deserted my post,
Though that was never my intent;

I swear
It was never part
Of any plan;

I was only lost at sea
With my true love
My beautiful Marie.

XIX

The ground was covered
With morning dew
So Earth's pain was being soothed too.

As I laid freed
By those angelic birds
That had taken refuge on my ship;

Such noble birds of prey
Pecked at the ropes around my wrists
Until the job was done that day.

And then in the misty rain,
I lay waiting for the sun again.
I laid there so worn and torn,

And I wondered what I had done."

THE END

ZOMBIE ECONOMY

#2. ZOMBIE ECONOMY

I

The invisible hand
Was holding yours all day
It didn't matter

You had no money to pay
So no one cared what you had to say
And the sun never shined

For you, Drew
And every day is a day of dread
Many think they would be better off dead.

II

Paper comes from a dead tree
But still in theory more worthy than you
So what can you do?

III

The visible feet
Walk up and down the street
As they move around the homeless

EPICS: Cloud Included

Sometimes the visible feet walk in a line
Sometimes slow
Sometimes fast

IV

And those with visible feet
Buy what they can to eat
Everything else is secondary

Cause surviving is the law of the beast
All connected on this food chain
That feeds our marrow

Even though this path is narrow
It is a step which must be taken
To start the game

Of Sum Zero
One can win so big
One forgets

Who you are
When you lose it all
Your feet will be still on the street

S.E. McKENZIE

Now so mean
A place that you have never seen
People living inside cardboard boxes

As you are held back, they will condescend
Still you must feed your marrow
On this path of greed so narrow

One must climb above it all
For one side will fall in the end
One side wins at such expense to the other,

And one way or another
You will be watched by big brother
In this prison town

V

Can't you see?
How this zombie economy
Shapes you and me

Fear destroys creation and innovation
Speed ups recession
Before you slump into depression

EPICS: Cloud Included

Panhandler is really a cop in disguise
Looks in the window of your car
So he can win a prize

One way or another
He is your big brother
Trying to catch you holding your phone

He gives out tickets
The faceless and nameless brand.
Is he part of the invisible hand?

VI

Big brother gives you a ticket
Now you have no money for food
But one way or another

He is your big brother.

Hey Drew, what will you do?
You have a brave smile
Will only last a

Until you get kicked down by the gatekeeper
One way or another he is your big brother
Though he does not know your name

To him everyone is the same
The strange combination of natural law
And artificial selection

Leads to a sad sensation
See all these fishes and loaves
Piled high by the mount
To share

When Peter could not be robbed to pay Paul
Market failure was felt by all
When the walls come falling down

Some won't mind
Others without walls will grow to be unkind
Others will close their eyes in fright

And hope to be comforted all night
In the glow of hope
Others will narrow their scope

EPICS: Cloud Included

For it is the way
Of the zombie economy
To ignore the chaos

The police state tried to control
The mounting loss
This made the masses cross

VII

As the visible feet
Kept walking on the street
Many of those feet began to disappear

There was so much doubt
And a growing climate of fear
Both far and near

And Drew's Momma said
Where are you Drew?
You should be in bed

Drew knew too
And his head was filled with dread
Couldn't get his foot in the door

To enter a future he was prepared for.
The world was on the brink of war
So Drew gave up too.

VIII

As panic set in
The wheels of the economy slowed down
People kept their surplus liquid

As supply and demand
Expected the invisible hand
To stroke good fortune in time

The visible feet
Were in recline
As the movement of things

Began to slow down
The zombie economy
Began to tip

Without a life line
Death gained its grip
And the promise was broken

As the pain had awoken

EPICS: Cloud Included

For risk was too high
So money was laid to rest
In jars behind bars and under the bed

Fear of fear and social unrest
Made it harder still
To build a better world

With more opportunity
So many were afraid to make it be
This feeling of doom divided society

There was the bad and the good
The weak and the strong
All hiding in the hood

Still believing that killing was wrong
The movement of things was interrupted
As a man with a gun stood at attention

One way or another he was your big brother

S.E. McKENZIE

Death and fear of it,
Was on everyone's mind.
So why care or be kind?

They all had to ask,
People are only themselves,
When wearing a mask.

The world was full of gloom and doom
Only love could make hope bloom
Paving a path into a kinder way.

And many stopped believing in love
Cause there was just too much scary stuff
There was frightening talk on the news all night

In the zombie way
Half alive and have dead
As debt dangled over your head

But then you drowned your pain
As you were stuck standing in the rain
Waiting your turn and it never came.

EPICS: Cloud Included

IX
The race is fast
Some will drown
Others will last

And win the crown
Some will need a life line
When no safety net is found

Others will be caught up
In red tape
While their visible feet are bound

X
Ride the economy like a bike
Keep your balance
And visible feet moving

Or the economy will crash
In the usual zombie way
And one way or another

Big brother will be watching you

XI

See the frown
See the malice in their face
While they bring you down

You must compete until the end
In this place, almost a prison town
Where streets are empty at night

They are that way out of fright
Barriers that block the way
Without any concern for what has been lost.

For this is almost a prison town.
Here you are half alive and half dead,
As the debt load hangs over your head.

In the usual zombie way
You must worry about who is following you?
When they drive around the block and stare at you

And who protects you and me
From this zombie economy
Sealed with degradation, alienation

And marginalization?

EPICS: Cloud Included

Easy for them when they can print money
And sell it back to the bank
Giving and taking away life

For that is the usual way
In the Zombie economy
That bites you until you bleed

As you roll on the ground in need
As you beg for your life
To be the best you can be

You are marked by the manmade beast
So he can feast
On your degradation

Half dead and half alive
Few are real
When not wearing a mask

One still must do the task
Needed to keep on living
Just to keep the hope alive

S.E. McKENZIE

A hurt sensation
When a hello would do
Alienation

When there is no love surrounding you.
Half alive and half dead
That is the way in this zombie economy

Can't economize
Only marginalize
But don't let them devalue you

Hold your head up high
Don't ever let them see you cry
And one day there will be a better way

With no war and debt to pay for war

No famine or suspicion of the underdog
No more getting followed around the block
Even though one way or another

He is your big brother

EPICS: Cloud Included

Once up in arms
So blind to hypocrisy
In the usual zombie economical way

Giving and taking life

Wastage and cruelty
There was no end
As data flowed it had to bend

Around mountains and through river beds
As debt mounted
The economy was given life

While the future had been sold.

In the zombie way
They follow a person around the block
But never say hello

Fear ruined innovation
So how could the economy grow?
Only through selling out tomorrow

As ambition was frozen in fear

XII

Visible feet were walking
On one side of the earth
While reclining on the other side

The illuminated were weeping
They had nowhere to hide
Their loss was tremendous

As data moved as fast as it could
Under rivers and over mountains
Data moved like liquid fountains

Dead matter fueled electricity so alive
While only the fittest were meant to survive
Said the one prone to illuminate,

What he said was final

For there was no need to debate
In the circle of the elite
For that would create more data to return

EPICS: Cloud Included

And some said that it was all a trap
The economy had crashed and could not move
While the visible feet kept walking the street

The motion was able to support and energize
As the beat of the skin drum
Was heard far and wide.

"Now what do you see?"
The man asked the bird of steel
The drone was alone

And had nothing to say
Someone was about to pay
As they toiled for oil all day

The missile flew into the air
Some said it was not fair
Others needed a sign

So they could feel free to care

As data was able to bend
There seemed to be no end
To how prices could fluctuate

Bottom out
Then bounce back
Like a dead cat

With nine lives
But none to spare
For there were missiles in the air

As money for a moment stood still
The crash was just for a few moments in time
As value of money fell

Prices began to climb
For some this was heaven
For others it was hell

EPICS: Cloud Included

XIII

How far away did you get
From the paper phantom of debt?
Did you fly away in your jet?

Was it ever really a safe bet
As data flew under river beds
And through tunnels of stone

The faster the trade
Higher the price
Before it fell

Into a manmade hell

Even though the ice
Was now liquid
And could flow freely

Many felt the gloom of doom
For one way or another
The man who was your big brother

Was still watching you
So how could you feel free
To be yourself?

Panic stricken
The visible feet ran out of the door
There were more and more

They all ran so fast
No one knew when the fear would end
Fear grew as the walls were falling down

We knew love gave us some strength
When everything around us
Seemed to vanish in thin air

When you have nothing
No one will care
Hey Drew

What will you do?

XIV

Fly the economy like a kite
Above all this bad and sad
Atmosphere

EPICS: Cloud Included

That is what you must do Drew
Before the game ruins you
With one zero to your name

Above the sky line
That you never see
That is where the zombie economy

Rests in food chains
So heavy and strong
And whatever you do to survive

Can never be wrong.
I hear the boots stomping
Enticing to let anger win, no gain just loss

It is our big brother telling us to move along
It is just our big brother
Blowing the whistle for his boss.

THE END

S.E. McKENZIE

OIL

#3. OIL

I

This tale is sad
But never intended
Peggy Lee and Stu

Had a garden which was unattended
As weeds grew out of control
A man knocked on their door

He showed Stu a map that was never shown before
Of many oil wells that were planned
He told Stu oil would always be in demand

For ever and ever
Which is always here
When you are rich

You have less to fear

II

The big machines
Toil for oil
Surrounding the earth in gooey spoil

The price of oil
Goes up and down
Controls the rate

Of currency
As price intertwines
With Peggy Lee and Stu's fate

Stu was told that the rich
Live better than most
Even though they may be haunted

By yesterday's ghost

EPICS: Cloud Included

III

The rule of tiny bacteria
From years gone by
Cooked under pressure

In a patch underground
Liquid catch
If all goes well

Will gush from the ground
And into the bank almost owned by the Cartel
For ever and ever

Or so it seems
As Stu watched in awe
As his cash flow returned in endless streams

That oil stream over there
Drowned Peggy Lee's dream
Her fear was awoken

Once Stu's promise was broken

IV

Black Gold
Under your feet
Black gold cooks what you eat

Black gold gushed into the air
Even though birds
Were flying up there

Black Gold could change everything
For a while
Could even make Stu smile

As he packed his bags
He was gone
To a land where money could buy everything

Except true love
That he had
Forgotten

EPICS: Cloud Included

V

Just another riddle
Ruled by supply and demand
Sometimes controlled

Sometimes in full swing
Fuels the engines of free enterprise
So loud

You won't hear the cries
Of the mother and her unborn
The steam hides the scream

Generated from a newborn's pure heart
When so many are torn apart
Peggy Lee clings to the past

As the future grew
Into a state unknown
Birds were trapped in gooey goo

S.E. McKENZIE

Tankers protected by flags
Waving in the wind
High to low pressure

Big machines dig for treasure
As they dream for black gold and pleasure
Until these young men grow old

Boom town
Brown ground
The dream gushes into thin air

Supply spirals but still in control
Crude pegged into a rabbit hole
As a man called Stu

Left all his eggs in one basket

EPICS: Cloud Included

VI

There will be a day
When prices climb to the sky
And then fall into the rabbit's dark hole

Volatile commodity without a soul
Finds a way to shrink
When all is wrapped up in black ink

Across the red line
The conflict can't be defined
No one knows what is wrong or right

Big rigs waving the flag all through the night
The red line defined
What was yours and what was mine

It was like the song
No one needed to sing along
For the music was designed to be listened to

When you were all alone

VII

That oil stream over there
Flowing through the pipe
Under the ground and waters too

Just another wild cat in the backyard
Owned by Stu
Became overnight millionaire

Always wanted to live like a sheik
As the oil gushed into thin air
It was black and it was sleek

His dream grew into what was true
Something that he could live by
Day by day

Such wealth gave Stu a new rank
And life too
He forgot that true love

Once kept him warm all night

VIII

That oil stream over there
Drowned Peggy Lee's dream
Her fear was awoken once

Stu's promise was broken

Her heart sank into the abyss
When Stu found wealth that came gushing out
Like a fountain with no cup to hold

The overflow

All of that black gold; so he left her
Broken hearted
As he departed

Stu had a new life now
For he had become a backyard millionaire
Almost overnight

Even though Peggy Lee's love
Had kept him warm all night
For many years gone by

IX

As oil fueled the economic engine
The demand for oil was never done
As the flags waved silently through the night

They were still waving under the morning sun
The newborn with heart so pure
Was dammed to fate

That black gold
Would dictate
As the war of words was being spun

The newborn's war had just begun
His life that was already on the line
Before he could walk or talk

He was given a toy gun
As the years went by
He learned to run

At the beginning it was so much fun

EPICS: Cloud Included

X

Love was a joy
Kept one motivated and fit
Kept one wanting more

As we toiled for oil
Oil gave us the steam
To fight for the American dream

Above ground
The pipes could not be seen
As oil was moved under the earth

It was clearly the supply stream
Everyone was hoping for
Would prevent war for land

That was clearly in demand
And was the very surface for feet
To walk upon

XI

The strategic goal was to foil
The opposition's
Quest for oil

And as the machines toiled for oil
The supply went up in flames
There were names
On the list to be blamed

As demand soared
Some called it an embargo
As the lines grew

As Peggy Lee saw the smoke
Took her bike
And rode away

Hoping to find a turn on the path
Of fate
Hoping to turn this hate

Around
Even if it meant
Keeping the oil in the ground

XII
How can you not fear
The scorched earth policy
To win the oil war

EPICS: Cloud Included

The oil lakes
On fire
You see the mistakes

Made by the power that is screaming
While the new born
Is scheduled to be

Newborn has no say
He is just so glad to be alive
And loved

Pure heart
Pure mind
In uniform by 2033

XIII
The spirit of oil
Was not free
How could it be?

The energy of fire
Gains like a liar
Short term

In the order of things
Oil is supplied
With all kinds of strings

Which become undone
Before the end
Some things when broken

Can never mend
With flexibility
Could learn to bend

Spilled oil all over the place
The demand cannot change
Until the price fluctuates

One side has supply in cap
The other has demand and need
How far will they go

To satisfy the oil god
Watching us
Burning in greed

EPICS: Cloud Included

Can you say?
Or will you lose your head
Can you say?

Through all this fear
The machines toil
For more oil

After we are all dead

The year without summer
Felt so poor
Though signs of wealth were all around

Frost bit at leaves
And bit at fruit
As long as there was gas for the car

Few really gave a hoot
They turned on the heat
And used more oil

As the machines toiled
People stayed inside
So they never saw

What had been spoiled

The sun's rays tried to shine
But the dust and smoke
Blocked its power

Peggy Lee wondered were Stu might be
She remembered how love
Kept them warm all night

During this year without summer
Peggy Lee hoped for Stu's return
Though she never heard from him again

She waited anyway
As her youth faded away
The flowers could not bloom

The frost had bitten them too soon

XIV

Oh can you see the cap on the well
It cannot stop the oil from gushing
Out in thin air

Can you see the machines toil for oil
They do it all day
They do it for no pay

They can't remember the time
When oil did not matter
When oil slept undisturbed

Without care or sense of time
Then one day the wild cat tempted Stu
And then the supply of oil it just grew

And some said that it was all a trap
Supply side to control demand to a degree
As price tumbled and fell

The scorched earth policy
Reigned
Until Earth became hell

THE END

S.E. McKENZIE

CLOUD

#4. CLOUD

I

There was a man called Dick
Who lived in a town that was toxic
Dick always felt sick

As he waited for the news
That was sad and gloomy
Wondering who he knew had been bruised

Dick was looking for a better way
But he never had a say
He hid from the vampires that drew blood

After they threw
Their neighbors' name
In the mud

There was no hello
All eyes were down
For Dick lived in a toxic town

II

Dick was always told
That he would soon grow old
So he needed to find the path in a hurry

That was made of gold.
And Dick always did what he was told
So he kept his head in the cloud

For that was the only way
He would not feel lost in the crowd
That was the only way

He would know what was allowed
He signed up for service at eighteen
He already knew that the world was cold and mean

When he was in the cloud
Dick felt like a movie star
He felt that he would go far

EPICS: Cloud Included

Dick wanted his life to last.
The years went by a little too fast
He saved his past

In the cloud
Some of the memory faded away
Some of it would always stay

III

The cloud was alive
Twenty four hours a day
And a girl called Jill

Found it quite a thrill
She too felt like a movie star
She was told that she would go far

So she didn't think twice

When her life became an open book
She would walk down the streets of ice
And get a dirty look

That was the price for individuality
That was the price for feeling free
The cloud was alive

For the cloud was powered by a super battery

IV

As the cloud ruled
It reigned from above
Data yours and mine

Flew in and out in time
At times it became lost
And crumbled in corruption

Dick could only whisper in frustration
When such loss
Caused cosmic interruption

"Where is my life?
It has been lost
This service was never meant

EPICS: Cloud Included

To have such a high opportunity cost."
The pages from years gone by
Were lost forever in the cloud

There was no fear
No human was near
And the super battery kept the cloud alive

As Dick fell to the ground
Dick was lost in a crowd
Dick couldn't speak too loud

Dick had no say
Dick had his pay
The money was stored in the cloud

Page by page
Dick's life faded away
Page by page

Dick had no say
In the process
That was run from a place across the sea

S.E. McKENZIE

Day by day

Though the cloud was stored
In that place so far away
The cloud's door could never be ignored

For the door to the cloud was in Dick's room
Where he looked for news
About gloom and doom

How could following such a path and direction
Not shape Dick's destiny
And fate's selection

They called him a bum
He lived in a slum
They said he was dumb

They left their garbage there
Cause no one would care
No one would dare

EPICS: Cloud Included

Oh do you see the pretty lights over there
Another street
That is watched closely

Another street
That the lowly
Are not welcomed or belong

As Dick fell from the cloud
And onto the ground
People came from all around

Some kicked him
Until he started to bleed
And all the good men

Did nothing at all
They just watched Dick crawl
He did not belong there at all

V

As Dick crawled home
He was just barely alive
Living in a toxic town

You do what you do to survive
Dick opened the door to the cloud
And then made a cup of tea

He hoped that he would heal
From his wounds
So no one could see

How he was degraded
And humiliated
By those on the other side of the street

Who had better things to eat
Better shoes on their feet
It was hard not to feel defeat

EPICS: Cloud Included

Toxic town
People wearing a frown
Throwing all their garbage around

On Dick's side of the street
The red line could
Only be crossed carefully

Or you would get run down
By those in a rush
To get to the finer part of town

Now Dick was always aware
When you came tumbling down from the cloud
He wondered if he would ever be free

From all the negativity and toxicity
That was thrown all around
And kept Dick down

In his toxic town
Where he always felt sick
Kept him in his place

The anger it swelled
And trapped him in misunderstanding
And labels so condescending

The anger it grew
And it made them laugh
As the joke grew crueler

Hate became the ruler
The thought police they were walking by
And looked at Dick in the eye

"What were you thinking?
When you crossed that street
You know they don't want you there

You know they will never care
So why were you waiting
For this world to grow more love

EPICS: Cloud Included

You must be soft in the head
If you wait too long
You will be dead"

VI

The cloud was as soft
As air
And it felt so safe up there

And Dick wanted independence
And to be free to be
Who he wanted to be

Dick had dreams
That were not in compliance
Some said they were an act of defiance

The thought police were everywhere
Some just stood there
Wearing a stare

For the next war would be in the air
It would feel safe
So many would not care

There was talk of cyber war
Espionage
And sabotage

Even though
Dick was just hoping for love
He knew true love could only be

In a land that was free

VII
The threat was real
And lurked from the cloud
Could be disruptive and was not allowed

This cyber war was misunderstood
While power was everything in a city
Without lights things did not look as pretty

Without power and electricity
People would grow cold
Some would freeze to death

EPICS: Cloud Included

Before they grew old
Then the journey
To find the path

Which led to gold
Would be put on hold
And no one would be told

The cyber war
Was classified
So no truth could be spoken

Even though
Many knew
What they were fighting for

Even though inequality was denied
All that was allowed
In the cloud

Was deceit
To avoid defeat
And the thought police

Were everywhere
In case someone thought otherwise
They would have to learn to despise

While looking into the enemy's eyes
For all was not what it seemed to be
This was now World War Three

Dick was not free and felt his captivity
Deep in his heart
This feeling tore him apart

He wanted to be free and independent
But he was told to hold the line
And be compliant

Otherwise
He would appear
To be defiant

And they would look right into Dick's eyes
And criticize
He was told the line to memorize

EPICS: Cloud Included

For it was now World War three
All around
There were feet stomping on the ground

VIII

During this war Dick had to be courageous
He was being watched
For any defiance could become contagious

The usual roar of war
Could not be heard
So this war was easier to ignore

Until the cloud came tumbling down
Broke into pieces
All around

Knowledge that had been passed down
Throughout the ages
Had to be saved somehow

Or there would be culture shock
One could lose the sense of time
Without a clock

S.E. McKENZIE

How could opportunity knock
If there was no door
Anymore

To the cloud
Where only silence was allowed
For secrets must be hidden from the crowd

Possessiveness could be an evil trait
And could lead to more
Conflict, war and hate

It was hard
Not to fight for possessions
When most of them were gone

What was left
Felt more precious
Easier to become more reckless

EPICS: Cloud Included

IX

The rule made it all one way
With no innovation or integration
How could there not be segregation?

The rule made it all one way
While the gap grew between
The east side and the west side

The door to the cloud
Was the only escape
Dick was allowed

For one must never speak
Or one would
Be disturbing the crowd

Privacy and identity
Went up in smoke
It was World War Three

In conditions of invisibility
Who was the enemy?
We just had to wait and see

X

Dick dreamt of a day
When love and peace would be restored
The more he dreamt the more he was ignored

Even though Jill felt the same way
She knew that Dick
Was being watched everyday

Jill knew that Dick could never be free
So how could love ever be
The fate of tomorrow

Was shaped by the war in the air
It could not be seen
And therefore easy to ignore

Until the cloud came
Tumbling down
And fell into pieces all around.

THE END

ON THE
OTHER SIDE

#5. ON THE OTHER SIDE

I

Once I was asleep in my bed
I slept through the night
Only to be awoken by an awful fright

The ground shook
And something roared
Underneath me

So drowsy was I
I didn't ask why
The rumble didn't crumble

The earth beneath my bed.
I was jolted from peaceful slumber
How could I do more than only grumble?

Now as I reflect,
I still don't understand
The power of such force

EPICS: Cloud Included

Was it the invisible hand?
So living
And unforgiving

Possibly the invisible hand was not living
Beneath my floor?
Possibly this unknown force was death

A body without hope or breath
Possibly a spirit floating by
Who couldn't reach the sky

But why was such force stirring under my bed
Why wasn't it
Stirring somewhere else instead?

Then I remembered his name
A man whose last years brought such great sorrow
Yes, such force could be stirring from Billy Joe

From days gone by
This man was certain
To not have reached the sky

And as I lost myself in thought
I just assumed
Billy Joe had turned to rot

The roar it grew
And the floor did shake
I was sure it must be his rage

Causing this earthquake
For his rage
Brought gloom and doom

Even though
His guilt was always denied
I always thought that Billy Joe had lied

He always begged to be heard
Even though
The world turned its back on him

EPICS: Cloud Included

That is how I remember Billy Joe
Though he always claimed his innocence
There was never a doubt

In most people's minds
It was Billy Joe to blame
For the deed that caused Mary Jane to die in pain

And that is why Billy Joe
Had not just been a prisoner in a cage
He had also been imprisoned by his rage

Until the day he died

Yes, his rage could have been stirring
So alone without peace
Still shackled and buried

Some place under the ground
In the abyss
Covered with morning mist

A legend from years gone by
Who couldn't reach the sky
For it is said he could not let Mary Jane go

To love another
So he took her life
With a butcher knife

A free spirit he could never possess
And how could his love be true
If he wouldn't let Mary Jane go

So she could be loved by another

II
Dead matter resting in eternity
Must be stirring, possibly
Hot mass deep in the ground

Made the ground around me rumble
I was sure the ground under my bed
Was about to crumble

There was nothing I could do
But only grumble
Hoping all would be well

Even though the roaring
Sounded like it was
Coming from Hell

EPICS: Cloud Included

III

And many would agree
And say free spirits
Can only enter heaven's gate

When they grow hearts free from hate

And others just can't understand
The tyrant spirit of persecution
For these men trying to gain social merit

Had no solution
As ancient spirits sought a home nearby
For they could not reach the sky

So they must join the chaos in the abyss below
For it had a greater pull
Than we will ever know

For the Earth's core; partly iron

Could warm the coldest heart
Even the heart of Billy Joe
For it was said

That he would rather kill his true love
Than let her be possessed by another
So he was trapped for ever

In his grave below

In the abyss, to never be free
For Eternity
For he would never reach the sky

IV

Beyond this civilization
It was said
Chaos ruled in the abyss

V

And some would disagree
And would sell you
Hope of order for a fee

Others would persecute
Harass and oppress
And then send the bill

EPICS: Cloud Included

To the critical mass
Don't ask why
And don't you cry

Just confess and self-incriminate
So you can fit into the mold
Which feeds all this hate

Until you grow old they will let you eat
Let those who persecute force you to kneel
Decide your fate without standing on your feet

VI

And there is no way out
And that is why
Some die

Before they ever lived
Some begin to live
When they know they are going to die

VII

Being awoken from my dream
I cursed this rage that roared
In the middle of the night

It just was not right
That a power from beneath
Had released its energy

Just to awake me
From my slumber
And I could only grumble

As I heard roars
In waves so loudly
Who else would have been turned to dust

And still exist so proudly?

VIII

If there was a way out
Of this hell hole
Billy Joe would find it

Yes I know

The force below the ground
Already knew
How to select and how to protect

And who to neglect

Gold, precious metals and gems
The need for them condemns
A fool to hard toil

Deep under the earth's soil

IX

Caught in the battle
Was never wise
For wounds would leave scars

That will be despised
Leaving you open
To being criticized

Scars on the mind and in the heart
Will leave you shattered
And torn apart

Just like Billy Joe
Who died in a cage
Engulfed in rage

Billy Joe would always deny
That he was the one who took the life
Of his true love Mary Jane

With a butcher knife

X

Where does this abyss end?
Is it is in space
Where light is able to bend

EPICS: Cloud Included

Or does it end
Beneath our feet miles below
Or is it in the heart when it learns to mend

When one tries to possess love
It will over flow
Just ask Billy Joe

XI

For it was said
Billy Joe would rather kill
Than let his only love be with another

XII

The treasures beneath
Had been taken
Many years ago

And in their place
Emptiness was left
Surrounded by moving plates

And artificial snow

And this was the time
The ground would open
Revealing the curse that would spread

Even in the space below my bed

A sinkhole hundreds of feet deep
Opened while my neighbor was still asleep
As he sunk into the earth

I was glad it was not me

XIII
The persecutor took what he could
And would have taken more
Until a judge came from the sky

And stopped the revolving door
With one mighty roar
That the wise could not ignore

XIV
I had a long way to go
After a hard day of work
Associating with those only

Pretending to be relating
Once I reached my destination
There would be a meal waiting

EPICS: Cloud Included

Once I arrived
I could put up my feet
Have something to eat

Always thankful that
I had survived
A hard day working nine to five

What else could I ask for
But an inside lock to my door
And to be safe

From polarization
And thoughtless chatter
So I could think about things

That really matter

XV
There were eyes everywhere
Watching those
In public space

Less privacy everyday

As freedom faded away
The force became less understanding
And more demanding

As the tides
Fall and rise
Private eyes see through the disguise

While stony barriers shape public space
The homeless
Had no status or no space

To call their own

Or so he said
When he saw them asleep in the study hall
He could only see red

As they were made to feel so small

EPICS: Cloud Included

No rights as housing costs soar
Lost rights as the force
In the abyss could only roar

Citizenship
Refuge
From hardship

XVI

As he wore a crown
Never his own
He had the power to put them down

In a world growing meaner
Everyday
The bill was sent

To the mass so critical
Who were beginning to feel
Hopelessly cynical

When books and things
Had more rights
Than you and I

We hoped for a dead man
To come from the sky
And to walk about and to ask why

We were waiting for a king
Who had no crown
We were waiting for something better

That wouldn't keep us down

So that we could live freely
In harmony
And to entrust each other

With our humanity

XVII

They had no say
And no right to speak out loud
That is why they were lost in the crowd

XVIII

This is the other side
Now you have nowhere to hide
Now you will get kicked down

EPICS: Cloud Included

As you try to get up
You had your cup
With coins that were thrown in

Not much there
Just tokens from people
Who tried to share

In a land that grew colder everyday
The bulldozers tore down
All the shacks in the slum

The mood between the elite
And everyone else was very glum
Only saved by their show of compassion

Even though only a show
Hid hypocrisy and deception
For it was the fashion

To despise what the eyes saw

XIX

People without disguise
Sleeping in the study hall
Was now against the law

When the homeless awoke
They felt so small
For they had no were to go

Where they could call their own
And were so alone
And lost in the crowd

XX

There were fishes from the sea
And loaves of bread
To share

Even though loitering in public space
Could open one to persecution
The man in the white robe

Sat on the hill with the solution
He began to explain,
"Your pain is my pain.

It will take a lot of love to learn to trust again.
In love we have so much to gain."
Then he saw the weapons

EPICS: Cloud Included

Of mass destruction
And he felt rage
"Turn these weapons into plowshares

While you still can
Believe in the rights of man
For that is the only way

To grow Goodwill."

As the crowd grew
The man on the hill
Divided the food and made it multiply

Many were too hungry to wonder
How this was done
They only ate before they were forced to run

For other men were arriving
Each carrying a gun
Then they arrested the son

Everyone cried
It was a painful sight
The good was lost

That was the cost
The whistle it blew
So what could they do?

For this was life on the other side

XXI

They took the man
And made him stand by a tree
They told him that he was going against policy.

"We are just doing our job
Controlling the mob
They know it is against the law

To loiter or sleep in the study hall
We don't care where they go
As long as they stay

On the other side
That is the way
Of today."

EPICS: Cloud Included

Then another man came out of the grocery store
And started to complain.
"You there giving away food

What world do you think we are living in?"
"I know," said the man in white
"This is the world of sin."

XXII
And where to begin
And when to end
In this world

You had to learn to bend
You had to turn away
While your heart

Tried to mend
For this was not
The way it should have been

S.E. McKENZIE

For it was true
And we all knew
This was paradise lost

That was the price
For the overkill
Of the underfed

XXIII
Fear of domination by foreigners
Made us trust the invisible hand more
As we all stood in polarized corners

We could not forget what had been lost
Made many of us mourners
While looking down upon others

Was not so easy now
As the man in white
Was still sitting by the tree

EPICS: Cloud Included

We were no longer allowed to rest in public places
For we were no longer free
Without freedom there was no privacy

The barriers blocked the way
So they could ghettoize
Many were too afraid to criticize

Many said these were the end days
As their negativity grew
So did their frown

But the man in white disagreed
And explained his point of view
He said evil would always try to deceive

But if we work together
There will be so much
We will be able to achieve

And love will make us strong
That is what we have to believe
Paradise is only lost

For it is buried
In all this conflict and tension
Beware of men of pretension

For they will be wearing crowns and jewels
Beware of these men, for they are fools
I am here to show you a new direction

Only way to stop this war
Is to learn to love each other more
While the tyranny of evil

Is all around

XXIV

We all need
Someone to feed
Dying in all this greed

And we all knew that was true
We just did not know what to do
For other men arrived, and each had a gun

EPICS: Cloud Included

Many of us started to run
As the man in white sitting by the tree
Stood up and said

The deed you do this day
Will never fade away
For it will echo into eternity

XXV

The persecutor took what he could
And would have taken more
Until a judge came from the sky

And stopped the revolving door
And we never asked why
For we all knew

The dangers on Earth
Could spread
To the rest of the galaxy

And the new world order
Was almost the same
It just had a different name

For it would take a lot of love
To work together and to unite
It would take a miracle

To turn this all around
And make it right
This is what we must do

We must open our arms
And welcome humanity
So we can try to prevent

World War Three.

THE END

WATER AND AIR

#6. WATER AND AIR
I

OH how it feasts
On innocence
Blank slate so misunderstood

Free from a guilty mind
Still pure and kind
Where intent and content

Invisible
Divisible
Never sustainable

You cannot ignore its roar
As it comes crashing down
Harder than ever before.

It cannot be policed

For it is the Microbeast;
It must climb the hill
And hunt prey to kill;

Food chain gets yanked one more time again

EPICS: Cloud Included

Oh how it feasts
On innocence
Blank slate so misunderstood

Free from a guilty mind
Still pure and kind
Where intent and content

Mutual beneficiality
Made this city
A long time ago.

That was the time
Of less crime
And exploitation

When everyone had a chance to live;
Until the arrival
Of the Microbeast.

Social power
Micro aggression
Macro suppression

What was once free
Is now in a cage.
What was once free

Burns in rage.
Must live his days like he is going to die.
Ignored intent and content; just a lie.

Touching him; half dead and half alive;
The victims of the Microbeast try to survive.
They hide every day

From their dictator;
They try hard to not become a hater;
Never too willing to give love a try.

OH how it feasts
On innocence
Blank slate so misunderstood

Free from a guilty mind
Still pure and kind
Where intent and content

EPICS: Cloud Included

Is so aware
How hard it is to care
Too late to cry

Living everyday ready to die
Even though there are still
New things to try.

Too young to feel so old
Too young to feel so cold
The Microbeast has its hold.

II
The big guns
Are standing by
Some are flying in the sky.

Negativity all around
Hate burning
In the ground

Never acknowledging why.

You can hear it roaring;
You can't block the sound;
For the Microbeast

Is said not to be just controlled
By agglomerates gone by;
It is controlled by its appetite

Which can never die.
Will fight until the end
For the right to rule and fool

Using fear to control and rule.

Through micro aggressors
And macro oppressors
Who need no vote;

So civilized they say
To bulldoze shacks
Of the have nots

"We do it to beautify"
They say
Those people will die anyway.

OH how it feasts
On innocence
Blank slate so misunderstood

EPICS: Cloud Included

Free from a guilty mind
Still pure and kind
Where intent and content

Built this city, a long time ago.

So civilized they say
To overkill
The underfed

We will make them go away
They don't belong here anyway
They were not born or bred here.

III
Ruling by fear
Took its toll
For the Microbeast was always near.

Mary phoned the cops on Sam
She accused him of being a troll;
She needed a man in a different role.

The canine unit chased Sam down the street
The dog treated Sam's arm
Like a piece of meat.

S.E. McKENZIE

And the Microbeast said
All power is in the head
So cover your ego don't let it show

So you will still have one tomorrow.
For no one cared
And no one dared

For the destruction fed the Microbeast;

It was such a feast.
Sam's arm could not be repaired
And his heart grew cold

Sam still loved Mary
And became a merchant of gold
Until he grew old.

What happened next
Was never told.
Their house and things are now sold.

Some say they went overseas
So they could begin again
Free from memories and yesterday's pain.

EPICS: Cloud Included

IV

There was an image
That was held up to the sky
No substance or life did it have

And no real person need apply
For the Microbeast
Would rather be alone

As it enjoyed its feast.
It was more true than true
And more real than real

The Microbeast
Could manipulate
How many would feel

Lost in hate.

They feel distain
Without refrain;
They beg the Microbeast to detain

Him; for evermore;
Ignored intent and content;
Inhuman Microbeast will now reign,

As tear drops fell gently from the heavens above.

V

For one; it was Laissez-faire;
And regulated for another;
Rivals could never be equals.

How could they be?
Don't you see?
That is how the Microbeast paves its way.

The Microbeast was in the heart.
The Microbeast was in the ground.
The Microbeast was everywhere;

While Jack and Jill climbed the hill
To get a pail of water;
As it rained the ground turned into mud all around.

Mud went into the water
And smoke went into the air;
Out of sight; Laissez-faire.

The water could not speak;
And the air could not scream;
Jack and Jill awoke from the dream

And felt so weak.

VI

Deeds done in the past
Will linger on
No one to blame, they had all gone.

Without water or air
The most powerful
Of all could only crawl.

Trees were cut down all around
A long time ago.
Now mud will sometimes flow

Into the rivers and streams.
There were a few cries of protest
And they were soon put under arrest.

We must stay Laissez-faire.
The politicians said before the voting few
You know who.

We are depending on you
To ignore
Those with less.

Oh how it feasts
On innocence
Blank slate so misunderstood

Free from a guilty mind
Still pure and kind
Where intent and content

Must stand strong
When the heart has been broken
And the pain has awoken.

So close your eyes
To inequality
Because that is the way it must be.

So you can have more;
There is no equality
Amongst rivals

Just like war;

And without earth, air and water
There can't be survival
Even for the fittest

EPICS: Cloud Included

As Jack and Jill climbed the hill
They tried not to fall
It was a long way to go for water

And they did not want to lose a drop
They had to water their crop
And they were working against the clock

For without water
Life as they knew it
Would come to a stop

Together they carried the pail
For without water
What was once strong would grow frail.

VII
Life is all around
In water and air.
It is just the beginning

Nothing much to do; Laissez-faire
Until you run out
Then you will scream and shout

As panic sets in
Many surrendered
They were too weak to fight.

For they were withering away
Some called it genocide
Others lied

And joined the other side
For freedom meant nothing
Without water or air.

Vulnerability
Fear of another
Oppression

Abuse of power
Over another
Hypocrisy

An act of war

VIII

A miracle of Nature undone
Around water, air and sun
Sacred combination

Of Nature and Nurture
Renewal in gentle sleep
To be deprived of Nature

Nature will take and give back
Yes, Nature will take over
That is Nature's way

Nature can force us to take a nap
Where ever we may be
Soon we will sleep in Eternity.

Jill stood at the mouth of the river
As the wind blew
She stood with babe in arms

No one knew
How she fell into the raging river
That fateful day

The Force of Nature was moving too fast
Rational Life Force
In action

Does it need to be controlled
To be sold
To the highest bidder?

Now Jack was half the man
He used to be
And his loss would haunt him

For Eternity,
He would never be free
From wondering what could have been.

IX

The water felt colder than air
Protected by civilization
It was a climate of Laissez-faire.

In another forgotten city
That time flew by
Too fast to understand and no longer pretty.

EPICS: Cloud Included

Jack paced back and forth
Lost in his sorrow
He feared the emptiness of tomorrow

Living in a forgotten city
Mud sometimes fell into the lake
An act of fate, result of an ancient mistake

Controlled by ghosts
From an era gone by
Jack tried to start his life all over again

X

Jack could see Jill through shadows
Descending from Eternity;
He wanted to get closer

So he climbed the tree;
For it could reach the heavens above;
Jack could not let go of his love.

As Jack climbed into the sky
He found a world
Much bigger than he

S.E. McKENZIE

Where piles of gold
Were here and there
In another world of laissez-faire

Beside the piles of gold
There was a man who was very old
And he was a giant of a man

His name was Sam

As Jack couldn't help but stare
Sam fell asleep in his chair
Sam snored so loud

It gave Jack a scare
But the Microbeast said
Think of the feast instead

Jack hurried down the tree
And left Sam's land
With a bag of gold in hand

As he climbed the hill
He thought of Jill
And cursed the river's chill

EPICS: Cloud Included

Jack felt Jill's aura faintly
Strong presence
Felt saintly

Who can I grow to be
Without my true love by my side?
Will this gold free me from all this pain inside?

XI

There wasn't a day
That went by
That Jack didn't think of Jill

And the pain never went away

The pail of water
Turned to rust
And in humanity Jack had lost his trust

The gold was good to him though
It gave him a new perspective on life
Because he now had running water

He had no reason to climb the hill
No reason at all
But he did anyway

Just to see Jill's shadow
Descending from Eternity
Reminding Jack that he had a long way to go

Before he could join Jill
Above the hill
Some still called heaven.

XII

OH how it feasts
On innocence
Blank slate so misunderstood

Free from a guilty mind
Still pure and kind
Where intent and content

Were not held under suspicion
Debt bondage
Next form of slavery

Without a plan
And little hope
How would the pre-living cope?

EPICS: Cloud Included

It was easy to convince
The lost generation
To tie the unborn

To debt from before
Like water and air
It was all Laissez-faire

OH how it feasts
On innocence
Blank slate so misunderstood

Free from a guilty mind
Still pure and kind
Where intent and content

Never ceased to wonder
As the Microbeast's roar
Could never be ignored

For it set the pace
And shaped the human race
Without needing a face

S.E. McKENZIE

XIII
The Microbeast
Will feast tonight
Under candlelight

Jack wondered why
He must jump over the candlestick
For it was quite cruel

If one thought about the words
Though no one ever did
For it was forbidden

To think
Jack would rather feast
With the Microbeast

And forget his pain and sorrow for a while.

THE END

SPRAWL

#7. SPRAWL

I

Saul's Sprawl
Urban decay
So bad everyone moved away

Not yet ready to let go
Of life
To give to another.

Saul; so trapped in his own subjectivity
He enjoyed his bias of negativity
Made him feel twice the man

He could no longer be
For his life
Was growing shorter

As the days turned
Into a process
Some believed to be

External Infinity

EPICS: Cloud Included

The possibility of another way
Defied the autocracy.
So let the good inside all

Pave the way to institute the Rights of Man

The one way autocracy wanted it all
Refused to share with other segments
Across the demographic range

Fluid and strange.

"We like it this way
For we detest disturbance and static
We like everything very quiet."

Billy Joe shook his head
And went out to check for mail
He was waiting for a letter

From his true love Sally Anne.
For he knew he loved her the most.
The mail box was rusty

Held by wire and tied to a post
Kept the property value down
Prime land on a river bed and so close to the sea

S.E. McKENZIE

The dictator called this an atrocity
And his frown
Was just the beginning of his ferocity

Ghost Town
Fear of the unknown
Slander and decay

No better way
To destroy
Goodwill

Of an old time city
Crashing down
Wearing a frown

Billy Joe and Sally Anne
Still found love
It was a miracle, many said

For Billy Joe and Sally Anne

Were living in separate worlds.
She promised to write
And he promised not to fight

EPICS: Cloud Included

As the old time city
Was shaped by hierarchy
From years gone by

Fear of the unknown lurking behind every wall
For Speed Traps were everywhere
No sign of what was yet to come

Old Souls from years gone by
Watched
As the ones who stood their ground

Hanged on
Refusing to fall
Back stabbing was replaced with sharing

Dirt and misinformation
Replaced by a kinder systemization
Which oversaw Idle Talk.

How important one feels
While kicking down another
Conflict between little sister and big brother

One way talk
As the Old Souls grow older
Almost dead but holding on to a string

They liquidate what they can
For they can buy anything
Before they die; too old to cry

Wearing a smile they know how to lie
Victim's hands tied behind their back
Easier to win that way they say

Of an old time city
Crashing down
Wearing a frown

Always putting strangers down
Speed trap
Money grab

Old Souls almost dead
So jealous are they
Of your new life

EPICS: Cloud Included

Their rage grows with age
How feeble they feel
Lost in their Idle Talk

The members
Of the Old Souls' Club
Are searching for a new pill

For they are always ill
And want internal youth
Contrary to external truth

Never too old
For a new thrill
They can still smile before they order a new bill

Sometimes the new bill
Will kill silently
Even though the Idle Talk

Grows quite loudly
Always putting you down
Wearing a frown

Puppet show
They think they know
The rules that make others fools

Feel the glory
In domination
So subjective

See those people
Labelled so conveniently
Not to dehumanize intentionally

But to objectify in order to control
Call them a name after their role
So blinded by the power it brings

Feel the glory
It will make you sing
Onto this steely thing

Of this blood sport sensation
Idle Talk
Misinformation

EPICS: Cloud Included

The truth more than opinion.
A fact not yet owned
And often distained and lost in pain

The need to dominate
Creates fate
Hides hate

The truth will be taken to the grave
The gate keeper flowing through the sky
Must filter so the spread of toxicity
Does not get by.

The keeper will see through hypocrisy
Will hold a place for judgment
And a place of rest

A place to see
Through hypocrisy
Spoken in Idle Talk

Deference to the old soul
Without a name
Roams through sprawl raging blame

Autocratic regime
One way power
Could only destroy the dream

"We know all about you,"
The ghostly voice said to Billy Joe.
"We will be watching you."

Sally Anne
Wrote a letter
That her Momma hid away

"We don't want you near a boy like that,"
Sally Anne heard her mother say
"Billy Joe listens to his own drummer;

And that is not the new way;
You must find a man
Who fits the plan

So you can be part of this new autocracy.

For we are better than him
In everyway
And we use science to prolong our stay.

EPICS: Cloud Included

II

Billy Joe felt intimidation
A new sensation
For his lost generation.

Idle talking
Idol walking
Winding up full of hate

Doing it to intimidate.
Obsolete City
Old ways that create

Fear of the unknown
An excuse for hate
Is so out of date

Feel the rage
Not enough to eat
Grows with age

Ancient city
Guarded by feeble minds
From days gone by

In a Land so rich
No one needs to be neighborly
Hate mongering, fear mongering

Transmitted by the speed of light
Put a person on the list
Spread the fear around

Never missed

Lateral violence
Micro aggression
Hysteria by suggestion

Condemned when condemning
Feud grew too intense
For Billy Joe and Sally Anne

EPICS: Cloud Included

To understand
It wasn't about love
It wasn't about land

It was all about following the plan
And maintaining control of power.
Forcing those weaker and meeker to kneel down

To the invisible hand
Never taking a stand
To protect the Rights of Man

III
Rhetoric replaced common sense
Poison replaced hope
Projection of the negative

Right through the wall
Very little space
In all this sprawl.

Social vampire
Sucked
Psychic fuel

Gave the social vampire
An energy surge
And social position

Revival of the inquisition

And the feud continued
As the rival
Exceeded all expectation

Count all your coins
Stack them in a big pile
Take a selfie

And let the memory linger.
Reckless with all his hate
The social vampire

Was never too late
Too collect his cash
To add to his stash

EPICS: Cloud Included

He would save every dime
Forgot life was all about time
Not just about growing an empire

While using force
Slander
And waste

The social vampire's youth
Was soon gone.
Now he was old and bitter

The social vampire
Vowed to never quit,
So he took a new name and hid.

THE END

ARMS

#8. ARMS

I

Hold me
You, across the sea
Hold me so I can feel

Security

In this land too expensive to be free
We need a lot more money
We need a lot more harmony

Not through guns and steel

But from arms
That will help us heal.
You know what I mean

And you know what I have seen
The world is full of so much heavy stuff
But none of it can replace love.

We don't need to flee
For we have already found
A land which gives us immunity

And time to beat the skin drum

In the downtown core
Prison city
No appeal to the human good

Easier to delete
With free needles
But no free lunch to eat

Buildings in this ghetto part of town
Were torn down
While status would always reflect what you could get

Behind this rampart
Of stone
You never felt so alone

As you climb the hill
Did you feel the elevation?
Or was it all in the mind

To be cruel or to be kind
To see or be
Willfully blind

EPICS: Cloud Included

So much need for power
Whenever there is fear
And there will never be a wall

High enough
To keep all the fear
Out of Bobby's heart

"The wall
Will just tear us apart,"
Anna Marie said

Before they went to bed
"The world is already so torn
What will it be like when he is born?'

"Innocent
And helpless
And in your arms

He will thrive
And love to be alive
He will grow and he will survive,"

Bobby replied
Hoping he had not lied
While Anna Marie cried.

And the rampart had to end
As the river's torrents began to bend
We needed a new guard

For the wall was not high enough
To protect us from this world
So cold, without love

Until the world
Was willing to trade
Arms of war

For plowshares
To end all this hunger
Which was surrounding these banks

Of gold and cold water.
Hold me,
You, across the sea

EPICS: Cloud Included

For we need
Our arms to be linked
So we can feel tranquility

II

The prison city was divided
No one wanted it that way
So Bobby and Anne Marie

Bought a chalet on the hill
The view gave them such a thrill
And no one knew and no one saw

How the fire began
The fire engine sat on the road
And was told that they were in

The wrong jurisdiction
And were not allowed to do a thing
So the authorities stood on the hill
And took a video

Of the fire burning to share the thrill

The video was seen by all
And everyone knew what they could not do
For that was the way of the prison city

How could this be
That they did not do a thing
Everyone was in charge

But no one had responsibility
They were just doing their job
And doing what they were told

As the fire burned their home down
Anne Marie cried
And Bobby's hope died

How could this be
Bobby asked everyday
How could we lose everything

So quickly that day
No one replied
For they were living in a prison city

III

Tom and Joe had a dream
That they wanted to actualize
So they rented a shop in the lower part of town

EPICS: Cloud Included

And put up as sign
The traffic flow was wild and free
For it was connected to the open economy

To their dismay
One day
A no entry sign was put in the way

Tom and Joe
Sat and watched
As the new store that sold the same thing

Opened down the street
Private drive
Made it right

The city officials said
A public drive was too much risk
Better for the traffic to drive by

As their debt piled up
The nightmare grew
Tom and Joe were no longer welcome anywhere

S.E. McKENZIE

The traffic flow was redirected
And Tom and Joe
Sat and waited

Tom's wife Trish
Had one wish
And that was to avoid being ruined

The rules were slanted
Against the poor
And everyone knew to lock their door

That official oppression
Was just a new rule
And to disobey you would be talked to as a fool

Trish was tired
And the her baby just grew
She walked to the river

And just fell in
And no one knew how or when
Heaven's door had opened the gate

EPICS: Cloud Included

Victorian Culture energy flow
Complacent and so eager to grow
At the speed of light through the internet

Oppressive but so ingrained
The look of sadness and inner pain
Was shared so only a few went insane

The pain was often mistaken
For anger and hate
Even though fear was so obvious and rampant

Controlled so many as paralysis set in
Possibly how Trish fell in
The river so unforgiving

Reflected reality all around
Nothing to work with
No arms to hold

The days of the old
Victorian Victory
Locked away in mystery

The historian had nothing more to say
All we could do was close our eyes and pray
Hoping for a better way

A cloud from the past
Made us doubt ourselves unless authorized
We were criticized

While hidden caverns in the ground
Owned by ghosts from the past
Dead but still could pull

The future into the Abyss

Without saying a word
For ghosts never spoke
And they never awoke

But what they left behind
From days gone by so Victorian
Could dismay

And Trish was with them now everyday
For it took strength to cope
During times of official oppression

EPICS: Cloud Included

Never out of sight
Could be seen
During a starless night.

IV

Hold me
You, across the sea
Hold me so I can feel

Serenity
For my land is haunted
By days gone by

And these ghosts do not sleep in the sky
For they rest below my feet
Within hidden caverns

Dug through hard labor during a time gone by

One day these caverns could reopen
And swallow
Whoever may be nearby

Their loved ones would wonder why
And would look for someone to blame
But no one took responsibility

For they were from a time gone by
A long time ago
A time of great sorrow

For many left their land of nativity
To find this place which gives
So many immunity

From the burdens of the past
Burdens from the industry of war
Burdens of servitude

To an authority
No one knew by name
It refused to take responsibility

Hold me
You, across the sea
Hold me so I can feel

Your arms of peace
Around me
Until the end of time

THE END

FOOTSTEPS

#9. FOOTSTEPS

I

As a boy
David walked beside his shadow
For his body was soaking up light

Which surrounded him.
He learned to gentlefy his might,
While showing Love to everything in sight.

He avoided every battle and every fight.
His shadow was invisible,
When there was little light.

He stood behind the tree
As Goliath showed his might
His weapon of war was to offend

Never making a friend; so willing to exclude.
Dehumanization; Group-think so rude.
As isolation drove the enemy mad,

Goliath knew how to be bad.
Fraternization was never allowed
That was how he controlled the crowd.

EPICS: Cloud Included

Life was better for the in-crowd
And everyone agreed
Except Saul

There were problems and hard times
Behind his wall
Because Saul didn't want to fall

There was mistrust
And fear of occupation
There was a thirst for a new sensation

And David cried out in pain
Let me go
So I may know

My higher power
Will guide me
To be the best I can be

Let my feet take me down the path
And during the night
The light will show me the way

I need those divine rights of man
So my spirit can pulsate freely
Regardless of the rewriting of history

I want to grow my mind
I want to be always kind
Never willfully blind

In the future years
Driven by my Momma's tears
I shall free myself from all my Fears."

And Goliath roared from behind
"Everyone is so small
Compared to me

I am a magnet for riches and glory
While I strangle you in poverty
And war so gory

For my footsteps
Create my path
And I will leave you in my aftermath

EPICS: Cloud Included

As I bring ruin to those behind that wall
I demand to see Saul
So I may watch him fall.

As a force of nature
I shall seal your fate."
And David replied,

"And without Love,
Thou shall be poisoned by your hate,
That is how you will seal your fate.

My real strength dear King,
Will be shown in the ring,
As I throw my five stones,

My footsteps too will create my path,
And I too will live in your aftermath,
And you will be the one to take the bath.

I shall unlock the gate of fate on this site
While His light in the night
Will show me the way."

II

"The path is mine
Cause I push and shove
You play your harp and speak of Love,

How do you expect to win?"
"I will win because His light shines upon my path
My footsteps are gentle and meek

Your roar is hard to ignore
And when you fall
The earth around you might crumble

But no one will grumble
For the Fear you spread
Will soon be dead."

"I foresee you under my feet
If you don't step aside
And find a place to hide

Let your king fight me."
"No, I hear the call."
"You must, I want Saul."

EPICS: Cloud Included

"No, you can't have it all
Just because you are tall
And I am small

I will go beyond my station
For I will follow my dream
Which has no end in sight

My feet shall follow this path
For I know how to bend when I see the light
And that is how I will mend

Whatever you may break
I will find your weakness
Letting it show, will be your last mistake."

III
Oh free spirit
How you roam
Do you ever crave a home?

You are free of obligation
Except to life
You have no restraint

You tear down walls
That get in the way
For freedom builds your might.

As the tyrant screamed out in rage
"You threaten my authority
And you do it in every page."

"Time brings life and time brings death
Time brought you your very first breath.
Time is forever but not for you."

As the free spirit grew deep in him
He was so afraid to be confined
By the cruel mastermind

Could not be defined
By the tyrant as he screamed
Watch the slaves awake

From their broken dreams
For they know the cost
Of never being free

For they are chained to the tyrant's misery.
Rewrite history
If you must.

EPICS: Cloud Included

As the tyrant pushed and shoved
David wrote poems
Of Peace and Love.

IV

Excitement of war is in the air
The tyrant wants that land
Over there

The soldiers will die in despair
But the tyrant won't ever care
He must have that land over there

The trumpets blare for the war has begun
And some will awake to the new day in the sun
Wondering if the peace will ever be won

Listen to the bell, for it will ring
Misinformation is in the spring
Close the freeways and all the ports

We will bunk together, in our humble forts.

See the divided world, it hoped for peace,
The way jilted Lovers hoped for Love,
But peace was just a dream on this field of war

S.E. McKENZIE

Drums of war electrify the heart
They summon feet to march in time
Before the enemy is torn apart

"Close your eyes and forget the past"
The king said very fast.
He sat on his throne

As commerce stood still
Able men were gone
Lost in struggle, goodwill was still feared.

No one wanted to be conquered
And were willing to die instead
The Fear could not stop, it was lost in their head.

As hostilities took heart
No one wanted to die
Time moved forward and could not go back

The manufactured hatred
Let the tyrant take control
"We must gain and maintain our dominant role"

EPICS: Cloud Included

We must prevent chaos
We are the boss and they are not
Let nature take them over and let them rot."

"Bury the plowshares
Never share the food
Let the enemy's hunger force him to brood"

The King said
As he sat on his throne
"Make the enemy feel isolated and all alone

Make him feel glum
So he will drown
In his own rum."

The soldiers wanted peace
And wanted to go home
They did not want war or to be forced to roam

Upon a scorched Earth
Trapped in no man's land
The soldiers wanted a peaceful plan

But were trapped
On land
No longer fit for man

For he knew no other way
To maintain
The free spirit that he was

So afraid to be confined
By the mastermind
He refused to be defined

By the willfully blind
Who should have known
The cost

Of never being free
He must step softly
Around this giant adversary

That opposes and attacks
That defames behind backs
Toxic vulture culture

EPICS: Cloud Included

Was all around
"You must try to stand your ground
If you can."

In a place where they love to ban
Anyone they can
Just for the thrill

The stress made their adversaries ill.

Toxic commodification
No concern for what was lost
Condescending and never ending

Made the steely tyrant
Feel in control
Like a chain gang boss

You must tread lightly
Around all this chaos
For Living Light will shine upon your ground

For silence is his power
So don't utter a sound
If you want to stick around

In this pump and dump town.

V
Free spirits roamed
On the earth before it was scorched and worn
Pages were written then torn

Praising the Earth's beauty
When nature was free and not just worn
Now nature is property

And lost peace
Raged as war.
What was lost

Was priceless
And no one would know
The cost

The trees were cut down
The waters turned brown
The ice began to melt

And so did the snow
The wild creatures
Had very few places to go.

The wild creatures
Were part of His Plan
Even the ones dependent on man.

One had to believe in the Golden Age
And then step aside
So that the green could be seen.

THE END

S.E. McKENZIE

DOORS

#10. DOORS
I
World War I wasn't fun
World War II well it made you
World War III is all around Lee

For Lee is a victim
Of what
He can't see.

Lee can't hear the roar of war
Though he has felt war
Many times before.

Lee gets up from his floor
And rushes through his door.
Making sure his hope

Stays intact
For bad vibes from spoken words
Are weapons of choice

In a world where domination
Of the despicables
Gain power from the reflections they see

Making it so easy to persecute Lee.

For reversing a broken heart
Is easier said than done
Overwhelmed by Dark Days hidden by the sun

Lee would feel despair,
In a world of strangers
Who pretend to care.

Fog is in the air
Droplets of water all around
Not yet soaking into the ground

War is destruction's rope
To win one must be
Never numbed with Fear

And Peace is more
Than just the absence of War
This has been said many times before.

Peace cannot be commodified
Though is often buried
In words that have lied.

EPICS: Cloud Included

Just like Love;
Recharges
Everyday

Electrifying and never in the way

Nature's Electricity
Creates light
Helps Lee see

Into the night

Sometimes Lee thinks
There is too much light
Until the fog comes rolling through

Mariana said,
"No need to shout
I am on Facebook deleting my friend out."

Lee knew someone had lied

Lee replied,
"I feel so much doubt
I feel there is no way out."

Lee and Mariana
Held hands real tight
As they watched the low clouds

Flow through the night

II
And the years went by
Mariana spent half her life
Deleting her friends on Facebook

For they all had lied
While she cried
Even though Facebook filled

Her emptiness inside.

And all through life
Lee faced doors;
Doors that could only be walked through

One door at a time.
Some would open
And some would close

Many doors could never be opened again.

EPICS: Cloud Included

Lee soon learned the secret of serenity
He found the key
To the only door needed

The door led to a room of his own

In a world
As cold as stone
Many would never have a room to call their own.

As the years went by
Same old doors closed in Lee's face
It was such a sad state

Feelings of disgrace.
Were replaced with hate
Only negative emotions were shared so freely

For fighting for Love
Was so out of date
So many preferred this feeling of hate

Faces were captured all around
Some so sad
They chose to be buried in the ground

How could his life begin
When no one would open the door
To let Lee in?

Lee continued to follow his path.

And the years went by
And many pages were turned
Many called the journey's path life

Even though many never opened the door
To the room in their mind
Their lost life was the aftermath

And their anger made them unkind
They were so trapped in feelings
Of gloom and doom.

Closed doors slammed in Lee's face
Were soon forgot
Only Fear could paralyze; leaving his mind to rot.

How could Lee be free?
No longer in charge of his destiny
Inside his mind there was no room

EPICS: Cloud Included

No shelter from his pain and gloom.
So how could his true Love bloom?
Love was now outdated and doomed to a tomb.

Lee turned away
The war was raging and out of sight
There were no winners

Even though both sides
Fought with all their might
All through the night

Peace could not be created
Between people
Who were trapped in hatred

And despair
How could Lee know true Love
When Marianna was never there

She was on Facebook
Deleting friends
Who had stabbed her in the back

Due to the loss
Each one felt
When they found refuge

Behind locked doors.

III

Once there was a mountain
Too high to climb
Until the ladders were built

And guides were willing
To show the way.
Once climbed

One could see the beauty all around
Above from the fog not yet soaked
Into the ground

The world was in danger
For the tyrant was ruling
With an iron fist

EPICS: Cloud Included

And narrow scope of vision
Made it an easier decision
To offend a stranger than befriend

Easier to hate the foreign
Confined affairs of others
By new legalistic rules written by fools.

And the evil grew.
So many lied and said
That it was not true.

When the evil grows out of control
The evil could grow
Stronger than you

So shut the door
Like you have done many times before
And don't be afraid any more

See the world
On the other side
Of this window pane

Not yet broken by torrential winds
And do you see who must hide
And who is thrown away

And who gets the final say?

IV

Lee and Mariana
Let time slip by
Grew a family

And as they grew
Each had a door
To their room

Which shielded them
As the years went by
More flags waved in the air

More graves were dug
Brave soldiers
Were drinking the legal drug in a jug

As time went by
Many would die
The ones left could no longer cry

EPICS: Cloud Included

The death of Hope
Was never mourned
And the dictatorship of Fear

Was followed and never scorned.
"Don't walk through that door,"
Mariana warned

"Without a goal
You will forever stroll
Under the control

Of that dictator troll."

"Thank you for warning me," said Lee.
"Don't wanna be perturbed and hated
Don't wanna live behind that door

For evermore.
Our life is the way it needs to be
For me to stay true to you

Our Love sets us on fire
And has freed us
From their power of Fear

And that power of Fear
Holds them all night
In a state of fright.

How can they love
When what they Fear
Is so anticipated?

Don't wanna be
Trapped behind that door
While their force feeds their bias so strong

Keeps them all so captivated
Without seeing the wrong
So tangled up in their war

Of words designed to fit
The late night culture
Ancient confirmation bias

Which was said to have trapped
The Dictator Troll's mind
A long time ago

EPICS: Cloud Included

And made him blind
To what could have been
Within a future

Not yet seen
And still an empty chance of fate
Free from any bias of hate

The future shall not be sealed
The ruler said from his throne
In a make believe Camelot

"Dreams cannot die and never be shot.

They tell you to fear anger
But Fear can make you rot
Paralyzed so afraid of being shot.

V

Walking through the revolving door
Done so many times before
Ghosts hidden in shadows

Went in and out for the ride
They were all dead
No need now for false pride.

Dead birds at your door step
Were thrown down the hall
For no reason at all.

In hope and anticipation
It was true
That tear drops blurred your eyes

Dark clouds over your head
Negative words
Create so much dread

Marianna's friends
Were not dead
Just deleted instead

Fear blinded the eyes
Too painful to see
Insight to future opportunity

As the dead were the very few
Who could still feel free."
Said Lee.

EPICS: Cloud Included

Negative words
Weapon of choice
Hopelessness numbed the mind

Love was worth fighting for
Love was kind
And no one would disagree

Trust could build Goodwill

But if not
One could rot
Under the battlefield

For evermore

World War I wasn't fun
World War II well it made you
World War III is all around Lee

For Lee is a victim
Of what
He can't see.

THE END

S.E. McKENZIE

WILLPOWER

#11. WILLPOWER

I

Wizard Steve
Sat on a stone
He was not alone

He looked to the sky
And he saw the clouds
Moving by

"Rise up from the cave
No need for flight
No need to fight

Always be brave."
Wizard Steve said
To his newborn son Paul.

"What gift does your new life bring?
Listen to your new heart sing;
So fit for survival, derived from a force so primal.

You won't need magic to succeed;
Good luck by chance is natural,
Beware of what cannot be explained;

For this is what you will need to know;

To prevent sorrow
In your life
When today flows into tomorrow.

But never let
What you don't know show
To the Sad Man

For he will take you
For a fool.
Treat you like a tool under his rule.

Always stay free.
If you can
Stay true to you.

And negativity is contagious;
People will think your positivity
Is outrageous.

So as you are squeezing my finger,
Let all your good thoughts linger,
For you can go beyond

What mass fate is said to be.

EPICS: Cloud Included

When the Sad Man takes control;
He will force you into a role;
His bigotry will sting.

He will lie; saying he knows everything;
And has a direct link to the Creator,
Even though he is nothing more than a hater.

Fear; his greatest social engineer.

He will kick you when you are down,
He will spread viscous rumors
All over town.

He will try to touch you with his steely touch,
He will always be asking for way too much;
For he will always be the Sad Man,

With so little to give.
He will always be the Sad Man
Trying to destroy your will to live.

You will need willpower,
All the time.
You will need willpower

To walk away
From this Sad Man
Who will try to steal your day.

He will seek to be awed in their worship.
He finds joy in gossip and other's misfortune.
He invades privacy and talks about doom and gloom,

Without thinking how we could all be
So happy
And free.

You must think higher
For the Sad Man
Will turn you into a fighter

So beware of this Sad Man
And the nightmare
He brings.

The pull of his negative vibes
Will be like a Dark cloud
Capturing you like a puppet on a string.

EPICS: Cloud Included

He will invade your mind
With words unkind.
His pull has a force; strong as a magnet.

You are not the culprit,
As he maliciously throws,
False accusations at you

In his double talk.

Walk away from his pull
For it knows no kindness.
Some call this pull evil,

For the harm it can do.
Others will let it through,
For they have no clue,

Who they could be,
If they were free,
From the Sad Man's

Negative Pull.

Not walking away from this Sad Man
Is your first mistake;
For he is a toxic man.

He will spread his dread
So effectively.
He will gossip subjectively.

So you must act selectively.
Hold on to your love protectively;
For Good Luck grows introspectively.

This Sad Man cannot see
What could be.
He creates his black cloud;

It hovers around his head
Through his negative spin.
He will share his dread;

For his hate tries
To control your fate.
Assumes the right to be the boss

EPICS: Cloud Included

Without compensation
He will lead you
Into starvation

Then go on vacation.
He will age in rage,
While you build your life

Free from Strife.

Your pain is no concern
To this Sad Man;
From him you will have nothing to learn.

He is drowning in hate
As he seals his fate;
Love would have changed this state.

But he is a Sad Man
For evermore
Slave to his narrow vision

He can only make
A simple decision.
He wants to be popular

He wants you as a follower
So he gossips his day away
For the Facebook crowd.

II
And the years went by;
Paul became a man.
Wizard Steve had taught him all he knew.

Sad Man
Grew old
And was buried in the ground

His name was soon forgotten
To most.
He roamed the earth

As a miserable ghost.
He continued to kick people down,
And no one could see his frown.

He continued to share
His spirit so unfair.
And his toxic vibes

EPICS: Cloud Included

Filled the air.
And for eternity and evermore
This Sad Man became an existential bore.

His existence created nothing new
Left nothing of value
Don't let that happen to you.

And this miserable ghost
Hurt himself the most
As his name was soon forgot

The worms that got
Into his resting place
Found that his core was already rot.

For the evil within
This Sad Man's heart
Was actually tearing him apart.

"Stay true to you
So that you may
Treat others the way

You would like to be treated too.

Don't waste your time;
For time is life
And time will fly by.

Before you know it; time will be gone.

Rise up to injustice,
Rise up if you can.
You don't need to put others down to be a man."

These words
Lingered
In Paul's ear,

As Paul grew tall,
There was nothing he would fear.
And he would never go back

To the days when he could only crawl.

III
Bitter Ghost
Roamed the Earth
And no one could see him

Though they could feel his rage;
Once a Sad Man,
Who gossiped on life's stage.

People would listen,
You know that is true,
But they hoped for a real friend,

Someone like you.

THE END

S.E. McKENZIE

BEAST

#12. BEAST

I

King of the Snow
Ice melting
Away his Life.

Beast
Roars in hunger
Hunger so strong

Changes the balance between
What is right
And what is wrong

The Food Chain unseen
Doesn't even divide
The weak from the strong.

As Life flows in living streams
You will never hear
The Eaten's screams.

The Food Chain
Links all Life.
Soothes Beast's pain.

As Beast strikes out again,
In conditions so harsh,
No Mercy can be shown.

Beast
Can't gentlefy his Might;
He must fight,

Even his own kind,
He will eat,
For he cannot accept defeat,

For he is not the only,
King of the Snow.
As ice melts;

He has further to go,
To get his dinner.
Life gets harsher,

Beast gets thinner.

Every day Beast must roam
For it is not enough to call this land his home;
For there are many more Kings of the Snow.

EPICS: Cloud Included

Beast's hunger is his Master,
And nothing more.
His Life takes Life and gives Life,

During a pace which just gets faster.

Up and down the Food Chain,
Of demand.
Beast's fate lies under the Invisible Hand.

And his killing is not about waging War;
He is just an omnivore,
And nothing more.

Beast's hunger grows his pain,
Tied to the Food Chain,
Pain that he cannot ignore.

As he roams
From shore to shore
His killing dims his roar;

For Beast is an omnivore and nothing more.

Beast looks back
To prevent an attack
He must stay strong

For all Kings of the Snow
Can smell Fear; as all scavengers know,
When Fear is near.

Beast can't gentlefy his Might
Or he will lose the fight,
For his Life

Is saved by the strength of his roar.
Strength to hunt for Food;
To sooth his hunger

He can't ignore.

Beast must fight for Life,
For he is an omnivore,
And nothing more.

EPICS: Cloud Included

II

Beast's sons are in the den.
Momma Bear
Is there to care

For new Kings of the Snow
Will one day
Make their way

Or die as they try
To earn their living
In the ice and snow.

So unforgiving.
See how the new Kings of the Snow
Play all day;

Their life is a joy,
The snow is a toy;
Though the pain of hunger

Will change their mood;
As they grow hungry for Food.
And the Living Food Chain Pull's again.

Their mood will change
In this land still strange
To the new Kings of the Snow

Will try to command
Or die as they try
To make a living

On their land so unforgiving.

III

Momma Bear is aware
As Man arrives
For he is the winner

Of every Battle
When he carries a gun
Often he kills for fun.

The bullet has done its deed,
Beast's blood runs out
Into a deep red stream.

Beast survives to roar one more time,
Then his life is done,
And the men ride away

EPICS: Cloud Included

Into the setting sun.

Momma Bear heard Beast's roar
Until it was no more
Beast was only an omnivore

And nothing more.
Momma Bear hides her young
As best as she can

For Momma Bear knew
That Beast had been taken down.
This land of snow for him was gone.

Beast's spirit was now lost
In Eternal Rage;
Black void beyond the sun;

Knew what Man had done.

IV

Jed turned his head,
Fell off his sled,
And Joe the driver had no clue.

S.E. McKENZIE

Jed
Saw Momma Bear's head
Poke out of her den

Beast had lost the fight
But Momma Bear's
Fight had just begun

Jed was still on the ground
As Momma Bear
Could not believe her eyes;

A man without a gun,
A man who had killed for fun,
A man who tried to run

Is no more.
Joe could hear Momma Bear roar
As Jed screamed

Joe turned around
And took aim;
And Momma Bear was no more;

EPICS: Cloud Included

Momma Bear was just an omnivore

And nothing more.
Now Man as a rule
Can act like a fool

Owns the night and the right

To the land
Is under his command
Man with a gun

Is the fiercest competitor of all.

For Man must win
For the hunt was deer.
The sound of guns and fear

Aggressor that will never belong
As the ice melts
Beast's sons

Run for fun
For they do not know
What had been done.

S.E. McKENZIE

As the Sun sets
Their hunger grows;
As Man defies Nature's rules
Death rang from Man's gun

And lingers in Beast's son's ear.
The one who died
Too soon;

Under the moon,
Without a name,
Who is to blame?

Man hunts in a pack,
Owns a lot of stuff,
No need for love.

Man has the power to rule this domain
As Beast's last son
Roams without a name.

THE END

THE THING

#13. THE THING

I

The Thing attracted the eye
For it was in plain sight,
Like a Temptress

It was forbidden.
The boss said so
And the cost would be Paradise lost.

To Eve's dismay
Adam ate the fruit anyway.
Some say the fruit's beauty

Led Adam astray.
Adam said he would not have
Lived life any other way.

"Feeling such pull
Had to be right."
Adam said,

Adam asked Eve,
"Have you ever felt anything
So tempting and alluring?"

EPICS: Cloud Included

"Yes, for love is even more enduring."

We must be aware of that Thing's pull
For it has the power to fool
And Boss told us to never break the rule

"Silence woman."
"Adam, we must take care
For Boss may force us to go."

"Eve,
I can't believe
That my love for this fruit is wrong

Look at me
This fruit
Has made me so strong."

"Adam don't you see
I need a gentle touch
Not a heavy hand

Show me the power of your love
And I will follow you
Across the land.

S.E. McKENZIE

I will stay true, I promise
Just stay by my side
Until life do us part,

Give me a gentle kiss
And I will be yours
In heavenly bliss.

Please don't go breaking my heart."

"Eve, I am stuck in a rut
Living with you in this hut
I wanna get out"

"Adam I am begging you please
I am down on my knees
Please do what is right

And I will follow
Where you lead
And all I need

Is that gentle love
I used to know.
Adam where did it go?"

EPICS: Cloud Included

"Eve do not grieve;
When I taste forbidden fruit
I am a stronger man

My faith is renewed in who I am;
And nothing steps in my way
Cause I am that kind of man.

So woman don't feed your fear
And give me space to breathe
I am who I am

And to that thought I hold dear."

"Adam, it is your greed that feeds my fear."
"Eve, I must be the strongest man that I can be."
"Adam show me that gentle touch

That I love so much
I don't need a heavy hand
For it turns my love sour;

Put down that forbidden fruit
And go pick a flower
That I can put in my hair."

I need that old time love
That I used to know,
Adam where did it go?

II

Soon Adam and Eve
Felt the state of undress.
Boss blamed the fruity Temptress

"Adam I was not kidding
I think we were too willing
To eat forbidden fruit

It was all wrong
Its pull was way too strong
It was probably stringing us along."

III

"Boss won't disclose his plan for us
For He is King of land and sky;
Adam must obey just to get by."

IV

What makes Boss
Think he is so elite?
Why should I say I was wrong

When forbidden fruit made me so strong?

Why should I agree to my defeat?
I am a man
I will eat what I want to eat.

I will not let such fruit rot
Nor let our opportunity
For empowerment be shot."

"Adam, I felt the pull too
Tree of Life felt so supernatural
And with new knowledge from that Tree

We now know Diversity

A chance to grow empathy;
For lovers with a heavy hand
Are never in demand.

"Eve, did you feel that tingling sensation too?
Whenever that fruit is near
I mean near enough to touch

I can't say no
I love that fruit
So much."

"Yes I did
And its power over you makes me fear.
Why did it have to be in sight and be so near?

Why did it give you so much might?
There is something about that Thing
Which was never right."

"Eve, what shall we call that Thing?"

"Boss calls it Temptation
Must be a tool to tempt a fool;
A trick of a master who is very cruel;

It was forbidden now boss will make a scene,
He could get mean,
Even scream,

EPICS: Cloud Included

For he is the king of the land and sky."

"Eve hold your tongue
And think of our young
Who have the right to this might."

"Adam, we shall teach our young grace
And to know their place
So they never question the boss

For his the king of land and sky.

If we prevent our young
From growing too mighty
We won't have to watch them die.

Clearly eating such fruit will be our loss
We were better off
When we obeyed the boss."

"Eve, It would have been
Another opportunity wasted
Just another fruit never tasted."

"Adam you know what we were told."
Adam interjected.
"I am a man and yearn to be free.

Eve listened
With disdain and dread
And then replied
I must see the world which surrounds me

I must taste its fruit whenever I can
So I can feel like a free man.
I know we should be satisfied

For we live in Paradise
How was I to know
The snake had lied?

Here good and evil do not divide
Snake said If we eat from that tree
Our Life may not end in Death."

We could gain eternal breath
And expand
Free from Boss' invisible hand."

EPICS: Cloud Included

"Adam, don't be a fool
Life is so precious
Because it ends too soon.

We did not need to understand
Because we were living Life
Under Boss' invisible hand."

"Such life is not for me
For I yearn to be free
And to see the world around me.

Now life is a rut
Living with you
In this hut.

I want to see the sea
And climb the ladder
To Eternity.

V

Son from years gone by
Climbed the mountain
Cause he couldn't fly

He found himself all alone

On that mountain made of stone
They said that one must atone
For generations gone by

And the son wondered why.

VI

The thing will sing
Praise onto the thing
Even though one day

The thing will fade away.
And all we will have left
Is life and time

Then that too
Will one day
Fade away.

How can we see
Truth and Beauty
Through all this Fog and War?

It is all around us
If we able to see
Life's living fragility.

EPICS: Cloud Included

Or if we do not see
It may be all blown away
By all this rush to fight

As death calls.

VII

The Lie grew
Between him
And you know who.

The Beast of hate
Shaped Fate.
The two edged sword

Was the tool
So cruel;
Gave power

To a fool
Who thought
It was his right to rule.

Hate grew
Between him
And you know who

S.E. McKENZIE

While Slander
Soothed his anger
For a moment or two.

The Beast sought power
Over the land;
He wanted absolute command.

As Hate grew
Hate began to cast a spell
Created the difference

Between Heaven and Hell.

And the beast wanted to rule
Everything in sight
For such power grew his might.

It didn't matter what was
Wrong or Right,
As long as he could win the Fight.

There was blood and gore
And he wanted more and more
For the Beast could not be satisfied;

EPICS: Cloud Included

So many died
And so many cried;
Some knew the Beast had lied.

This was the Age of Rage
While only Slander
Could soothe his anger

For a moment or two
Until he even tried
To target you.

He built
The Thing;
A new one every day

And he killed
Anyone
Who got in the way.

The power
Was organic and cosmic
Felt glorious and orgasmic

He praised the thing;
He sung to the thing;
He became one with the thing.

And he wanted more.
The Beast grew;
As his hate was consumed

In this land where love once bloomed.
The Beast didn't care
Who was doomed;

His word was not designed
To better humanity
For his word

Was the tool of Slander

Soothed his anger
For a moment or two.
And the Beast said

"Take power
Any way you can,
For that is how

EPICS: Cloud Included

You will feel like a man."
And the Beast could not care
For he was just a fool.

He craved glory
And made up the rule
Behind walls to divide and conquer

The Saboteur used Slander
For it soothed his anger
For a minute or two.

And the son asked
"What should I do?"
And the old man replied

You must reach higher
Than the fighter
Dodge his negativity anyway you can

Only when you win
You will be treated
Like a man.

Show the world some positivity
Then your light
Will shine

Upon the path you must follow

So do not avenge me
Make me proud
And go beyond

The narrow minded vision.
Don't be a tool for a fool
Make a better decision.

VIII

Gentle child
Knew the path
For he took it every day

Until a monster-truck
Had parked in the way
Giving gentle child no right of way.

IX

Wild Spirit
Vital and principal force
In all living matter

EPICS: Cloud Included

When broken
One is sadder
Some say badder

Walk away
To avoid being a target
A direct hit

As Toxic Man roams
He leaves widows
And burns homes

So many had fallen
Never knowing his name,
There was no one to blame?

No one at all.
It is up to you
To not fall

During this urban war
No one cares
Who you are.

Toxic man
Talks, doesn't he love to talk
About equalization

But all there was
Was separation
A hurt sensation

For the last generation.

X

The young
Searched for truth
The innocence of youth

Was no more; they realized
The one they loved
Had lied.

And how they cried
When the promise was broken;
They ran into the crowd.

Bullets were flying all around
Many were shot
And had fallen down.

EPICS: Cloud Included

As the young were dying on the ground
The Wild Spirit
Flew in the wind.

And the Wild Spirit
Knew what had been done.
And the pain it grew

XI

There was no limit
To the power
The Wild Spirit knew

Even though
Toxic Man owned
Almost everything in sight

Toxic Man was no match
For Wild Spirit's
Might

So there was no freedom to be had.
Some felt sad
Many went bad.

Toxic man
Showed his bias proudly
His pride was shared loudly.

Toxic man;
Just another sad man
Who steps in the way

.

XII
And I saw mercy
Crying through all our fear
For mercy tried to give

But Toxic Man
Would not allow
Mercy to live.

XIII
Toxic man
Lives beneath
Wild Spirit

EPICS: Cloud Included

And above the fallen
Youth
Had been stolen

Now
Sad ghosts
Surround this ground

XIV

Bias grew the way it knew
So Toxic Man was pulled too
And became trapped in his frame of mind

After he built this city
So pretty on a hill
Night time lights lit up

Promising a thrill
In his hand-me down town;
Time past it by.

Victorian age was left
For it made so many cry
Others fought to live

S.E. McKENZIE

Until it was their time to die.
Like the fruit on the tree
Fermented and pretty

Time wilted most things its true
Even me and you
Found glory in our love so true.

A time to live and a time to die
In this hand-me down city
Where most just drive by.

Souls were fenced in but not yet lost
They were just victims
Of a hidden opportunity cost.

Toxic man was surrounded
By the fake and snooty
He forgot about true love's beauty

That glowed in the night
Felt so right
Shone so bright.

EPICS: Cloud Included

Toxic man never questioned his loss;
So grateful was he
To be the boss.

Forgotten garden
From a long time ago
Was still home to ancient snakes

Who understood
Toxic man's mistakes.
The snakes could see the growing plumes,

They could smell the poisonous fumes.

Toxic man never knew
What he was fighting for
Until his fight was lost.

He returned to Wild Spirit that Day
And was granted new life as a bird
And then he flew away.

Never to be
An angel with wings
For he had been fooled by deadly things.

THE END

GRAB IT

#14. GRAB IT

I

Grabber knew when Elaine was down
For rumors were spread all over town.
Grabber knew when to pounce.

Elaine could not run
Nor bounce
Back into the life

That Grabber turned upside down.

Grabber
Spoke softly so Elaine could not hear
The fear of souls gone by.

The ones no one heard
When they cried out in pain
No one came

For there was no love in sight
Very few could free themselves
From their fright.

Grabber knew military prestige
While Elaine was too naïve.
To learn fast.

That Grabber's smile would never last.

Fear so cold
Froze many in time
Until they grew old.

Grabber was wearing a smile
When he said that he would
Be around for a while,

Even after those others were gone.

Some mourned those missing last words
Now blunted swords of the mighty
For No one knew where they had gone.

And Elaine had no reason
To feel intimidated
While she was being initiated.

Grabber was overjoyed
When she said that she was not paranoid
Grabber was so elite no one could call him schizoid.

EPICS: Cloud Included

Before he popped a steroid
And then shook his index finger
He faked not being annoyed

And he let this persona linger.

For Elaine was young and able
To work for free
For this was the new economy

The Cashless Society
Polarized in a mean way
Two sides fit together one way

And the grabber knew who to accuse
And he knew who to abuse
And he knew who to use.

Before he pulled out his gun
Some knew when to run
And leave all behind

For the land one day
Would grow back into nature;
And that hole in the wall

Would become a perfect nest
For a beautiful bird
Some would call a pest.

The Grabber never knew what was best
And saw the savage
In what was wild

The Grabber grew old
Day by day
While he put tons of cash away.

Grabber would splash cash before the smash
And how he loved to consume
Tons of energy from people he never knew.

And that energy might renew
Into something new
And that was the best that Grabber could do.

And no one could ever be
Another Elaine
Or really ever understand her pain.

And how Grabber tried
To make a clone
Out of you too

EPICS: Cloud Included

Before he grabbed land to pave
Over her grave there was a fence.
He said that a fence was his best defense.

What grew behind it was fodder for comics
Tragedy called new world order
So good for global economics

And power was nurtured so it could grow
Into a machine of sorrow
Within their dread, many faced tomorrow

When bad, the other side of good was turned around.

And in the end
Elaine's only friend
Was that bird living in a hole in a wall.

As you opened your door
He would sing to you and her every day;
A hello that brought cheer and was true

To yourself you must be
For all these things from days gone by
Will turn to rust and fade away; one day;

S.E. McKENZIE

As the grabber grew an invisible hand

"Money gave too much power to the underclass,"
Said the plutocrat
"Money would make them feel too much like an aristocrat

And imagine not knowing that
Or how to be a tool for a fool
That is why old school needs to be more cruel."

And Grabber said
"If you want to eat
Feel defeat

And kneel at my feet."
And Grabber knew Money grew in value
As demand grew out of hand.

Money gave freedom
And independence
From the plutocrat's command

For a few hours a day
Freedom from feudalistic
Never mystic; Society.

EPICS: Cloud Included

"And who is your Lord?"
Grabber asked.
"It is me, Lord of the land.

Sometimes called the invisible hand?
As Money was piling up inside Grabber's drawer
He took yours too before he left slamming your door.

He was so annoyed
Cause you were self-employed
And he wanted to return to cashless slavery

When he felt so much bravery.

In this new Economy
The age of the Cashless Society
Where everything was only free

Until you wanted more.

Grabber knew how to manipulate
Twist words around and control fate
And he knew how the oppressed loved to hate.

He never had to order the mass to behave
For the frame; all around their mind;
Shaped them to grow unkind.

S.E. McKENZIE

In the old world, in a land so far away
There was a mass grave that Grabber hid under
Another man's blunder

The anger was heard from afar
And thunder's rumble was the sound
As lightning's spark hit the ground

To make this land more fertile

II

Black bird with yellow beak
What would you say if you could speak?
You carried a twig

For your nest
But the tree was now gone
Your nest was not seen

Your eggs were crushed
It was unforeseen
No one did it to be mean.

The negative bias
Let Grabber hide
Behind his Alias

EPICS: Cloud Included

But the black bird with the yellow beak
Was not fooled
He dropped his twig

And sang a tune
It was so sad
It brought a tear to my eye

Grabber did not care
For he had already chopped his wood
That is why the bird's tree was no longer there

And many said that the flood began
For Grabber never gave thanks
Even when the flood raged above its banks.

And it rained day after day
And there was too much rain
To soak into the ground

Where Elaine's friends were hidden
For it was forbidden
To hear ghosts speak

S.E. McKENZIE

And as the waters rose
The dam burst and came tumbling down
For the dam was above capacity

The flood was called another unforeseen tragedy
While this water so pure
Grew the wild forest that we all knew

As the water fed these living streams
The people were drowning
Amidst the sound of screams

Elaine could not feel their pain
While Grabber turned away
He had nothing to say

Though his greed
Freed
The deadliest force

The world had ever seen.

EPICS: Cloud Included

III

As the hard line even got harder
Black bird with yellow beak
Looked all around but couldn't speak

Grabber didn't care about consent
All he wanted was his rent
And he didn't have much time to grow his content

And black bird with yellow beak
Flew in the sky so free
Then stopped to rest in a weed

That one day would grow into another tree.

And house black bird and his family
While Grabber had no time to feel empty
For there was so much for him to gain

As long as he closed his eyes
To all our pain.
As the barriers he built were beautified

We all knew that Grabber had lied
And if we weren't so petrified
We would have tried

To hear the voices that could not be heard;
So far away and underground;
They were out of the way;

Their faint echo can still be heard today.

THE END

Produced by S.E. McKenzie Productions
First Print Edition April 2015

Enquiries: 1(778)992-2453
Mailing Address:
S. E. McKenzie Productions
168 B 5th St.
Courtenay, BC
V9N 1J4

Email Address:
messidartha@aol.com

http://www.amazon.com/SarahMcKenzie/e/B00H9RWX48/ref=ntt_dp_epw

www.ingramcontent.com/pod-product-compliance
Lightning Source LLC
Chambersburg PA
CBHW061818040426
42447CB00012B/2708